Cross Stitch
Five Seasons
of Quilts

4

7

10

13

Designs by Ursula Michael

16

LEISURE ARTS, INC. • Little Rock, Arkansas

Spring Quilts

Featuring bright shades captured in a cheerful display of patchwork quilts, this design will bring a burst of color to your home this spring.

Stitch Count = 256w × 67h

FABRIC SIZE
- One 27" x 10" (68.6cm x 25.4cm) piece of 28-ct. White Jazlyn® by Zweigart® (stitched over two threads)

DESIGN SIZE
- 25-ct. = 20½" × 5⅜" (52.1cm × 13.7cm)
- 28-ct. = 18¼" × 4¾" (46.4cm × 12.1cm)
- 32-ct. = 16" × 4⅛" (40.6cm × 10.5cm)

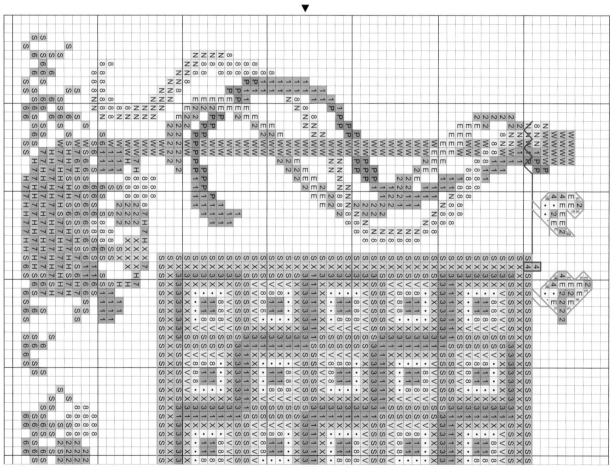

CROSS STITCH			
ANCHOR	DMC		COLOR
002	•	White	White
240	V	164	Light Forest Green
110	3	208	Very Dark Lavender
108	X	210	Medium Lavender
293	8	727	Very Light Topaz
024	O	776	Medium Pink
131	2	798	Dark Delft Blue
130	E	809	Delft Blue
027	1	894	Very Light Carnation

CROSS STITCH			
ANCHOR	DMC		COLOR
920	W	932	Light Antique Blue
297	N	973	Bright Canary
363	H	977	Light Golden Brown
246	6	986	Very Dark Forest Green
242	S	989	Forest Green
328	4	3341	Apricot
365	7	3826	Golden Brown
029	P	3831	Dark Raspberry
1090	Z	3846	Light Bright Turquoise

BACKSTITCH			
ANCHOR	DMC		COLOR
131	——	798	Dark Delft Blue
246	——	986	Very Dark Forest Green
029	——	3831	Dark Raspberry

Gray area indicates last row of previous section of design.

4

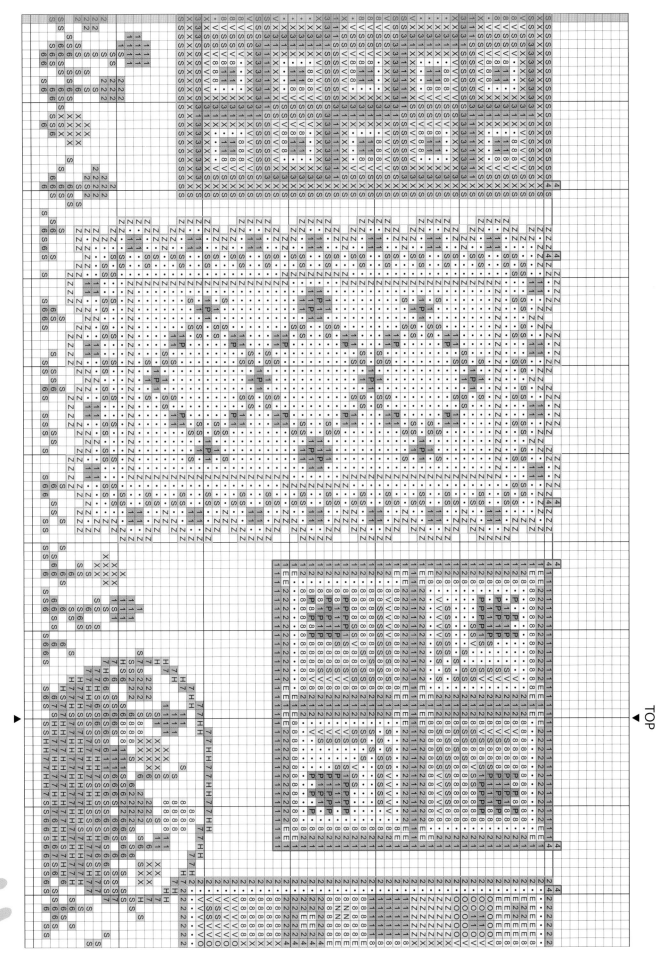

Summer Quilts

Bring a ray of sunshine to your home! This vibrant design features the colors of summer captured in a sandy beach display of patchwork quilts.

Stitch Count = 290w × 78h

FABRIC SIZE
- One 27" x 10" (68.6cm × 25.4cm) piece of 28-ct. White Jazlyn® by Zweigart® (stitched over two threads)

DESIGN SIZE
- 25-ct. = 23¼" × 6¼" (59.1cm × 15.9cm)
- 28-ct. = 20⅝" × 5½" (52.4cm × 14.0cm)
- 32-ct. = 18⅛" × 4⅞" (46.0cm × 12.4cm)

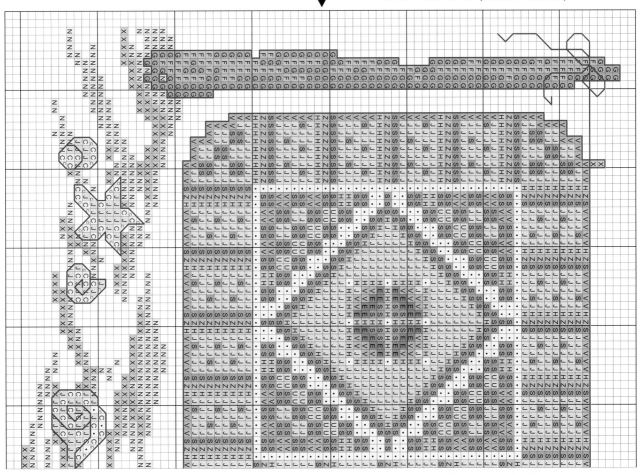

CROSS STITCH

ANCHOR		DMC	COLOR
001	•	B5200	Snow White
403	S	310	Black
9046	V	321	Christmas Red
943	X	422	Light Hazelnut Brown
290	R	444	Dark Lemon
288	C	445	Light Lemon
903	G	640	Very Dark Beige Gray
245	Z	701	Light Christmas Green
238	H	703	Chartreuse
942	N	738	Very Light Tan

CROSS STITCH

ANCHOR		DMC	COLOR
259	U	772	Very Light Yellow Green
307	L	783	Medium Topaz
133	T	796	Dark Royal Blue
022	E	815	Medium Garnet
160	P	827	Very Light Blue
944	M	869	Very Dark Hazelnut Brown
033	J	892	Medium Carnation
433	A	996	Medium Electric Blue
899	F	3782	Light Mocha Brown

BACKSTITCH

ANCHOR		DMC	COLOR
403	——	310	Black

▨ Gray area indicates last row of previous section of design.

7

TOP

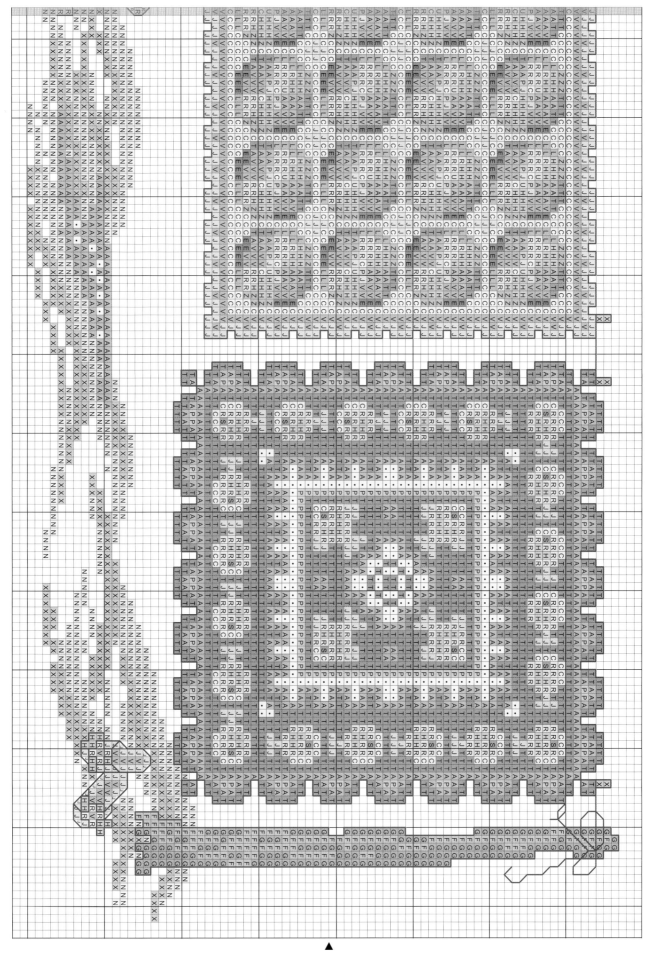

Autumn Quilts

The warm colors of autumn are captured in a heartwarming display of patchwork quilts and are sure to stir up feelings of a crisp fall afternoon.

Stitch Count = 277w × 74h

FABRIC SIZE
- One 27" × 10" (68.6cm × 25.4cm) piece of 28-ct. Bone Jazlyn® by Zweigart® (stitched over two threads)

DESIGN SIZE
- 25-ct. = 22⅛" × 6" (56.2cm × 15.2cm)
- 28-ct. = 19¾" × 5¼" (50.2cm × 13.3cm)
- 32-ct. = 17⅜" × 4⅝" (44.1cm × 11.7cm)

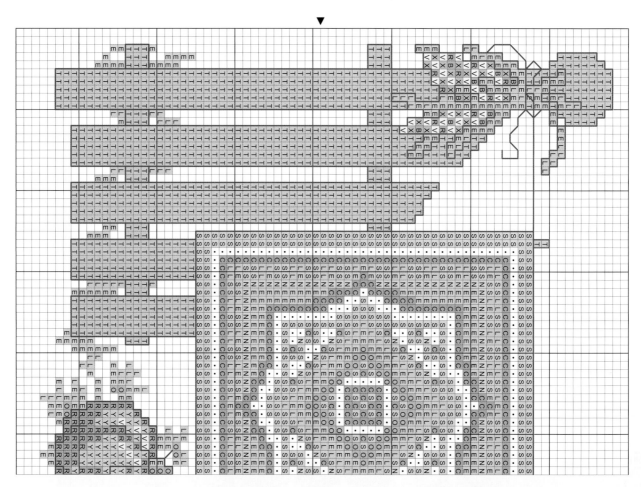

CROSS STITCH			
ANCHOR		DMC	COLOR
001	·	B5200	Snow White
979	J	312	Very Dark Baby Blue
9046	S	321	Christmas Red
977	Z	334	Medium Baby Blue
011	H	350	Medium Coral
1046	K	435	Very Light Brown
362	A	437	Light Tan
267	E	470	Light Avocado Green

CROSS STITCH			
ANCHOR		DMC	COLOR
265	L	471	Very Light Avocado Green
326	R	720	Dark Orange Spice
316	Y	740	Tangerine
307	X	783	Medium Topaz
022	C	815	Medium Garnet
269	O	936	Very Dark Avocado Green
382	B	3371	Black Brown
899	T	3782	Light Mocha Brown

CROSS STITCH			
ANCHOR		DMC	COLOR
305	N	3821	Straw
295	V	3822	Light Straw
976	F	3841	Pale Baby Blue

BACKSTITCH		
ANCHOR	DMC	COLOR
382 ——	3371	Black Brown

▦ Gray area indicates last row of previous section of design.

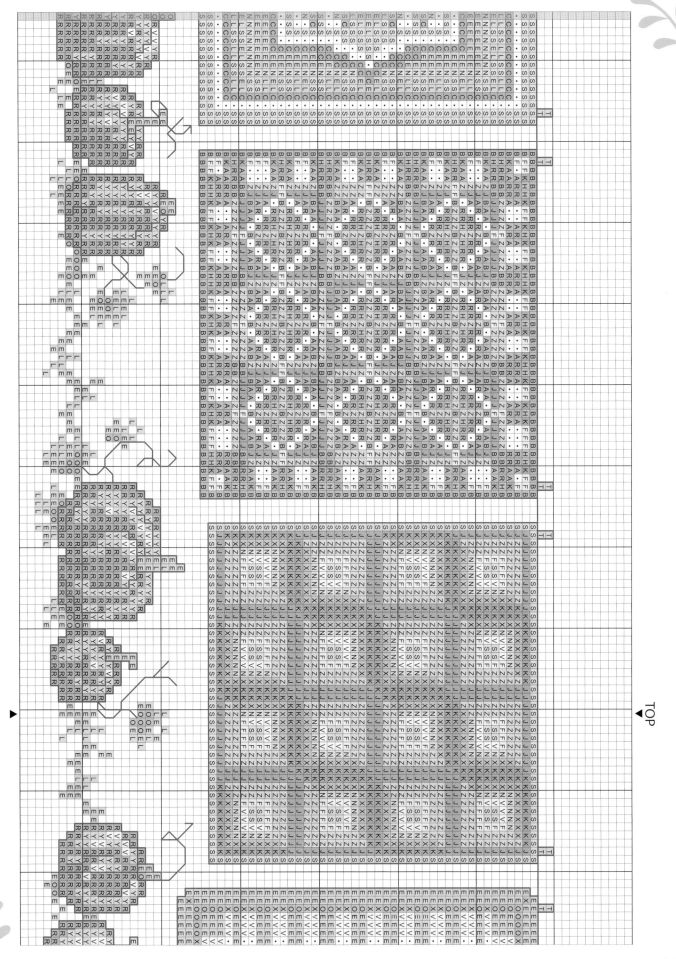

TOP

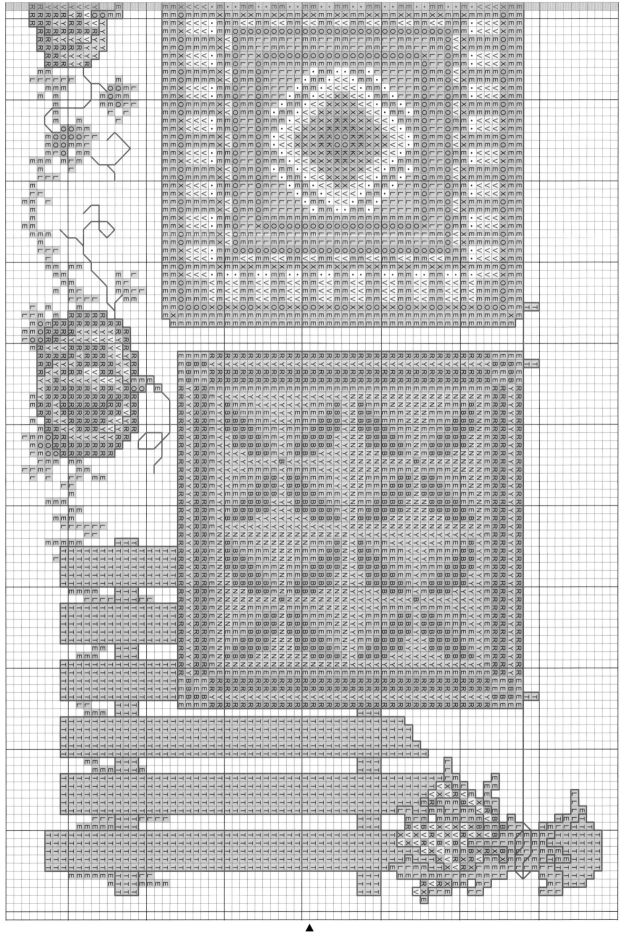

Winter Quilts

The cool colors of winter are reflected in this display of patchwork quilts. The charming design makes a great addition to your home all winter long.

Stitch Count = 264w × 68h

FABRIC SIZE
- One 27" x 10" (68.6cm x 25.4cm) piece of 28-ct. Mushroom Jazlyn® by Zweigart® (stitched over two threads)

DESIGN SIZE
- 25-ct. = 21⅛" x 5½" (53.7cm x 14.0cm)
- 28-ct. = 18⅞" x 4⅞" (47.9cm x 12.4cm)
- 32-ct. = 16½" x 4¼" (41.9cm x 10.8cm)

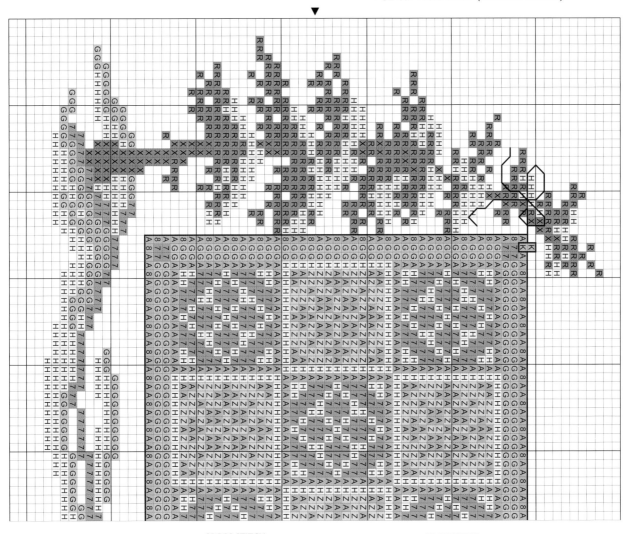

CROSS STITCH

ANCHOR		DMC	COLOR
002	H	White	White
110	8	208	Very Dark Lavender
108	F	210	Medium Lavender
211	S	505	Jade
210	2	562	Medium Jade
208	T	563	Light Jade
293	V	727	Very Light Topaz
128	Z	775	Very Light Baby Blue

CROSS STITCH

ANCHOR		DMC	COLOR
132	7	797	Royal Blue
359	X	801	Dark Coffee Brown
130	G	809	Delft Blue
134	A	820	Very Dark Royal Blue
269	R	936	Very Dark Avocado Green
306	K	3820	Dark Straw
1089	5	3843	Electric Blue
1090	N	3846	Light Bright Turquoise

BACKSTITCH

ANCHOR		DMC	COLOR
134	——	820	Very Dark Royal Blue

☐ Gray area indicates last row of previous section of design.

13

TOP

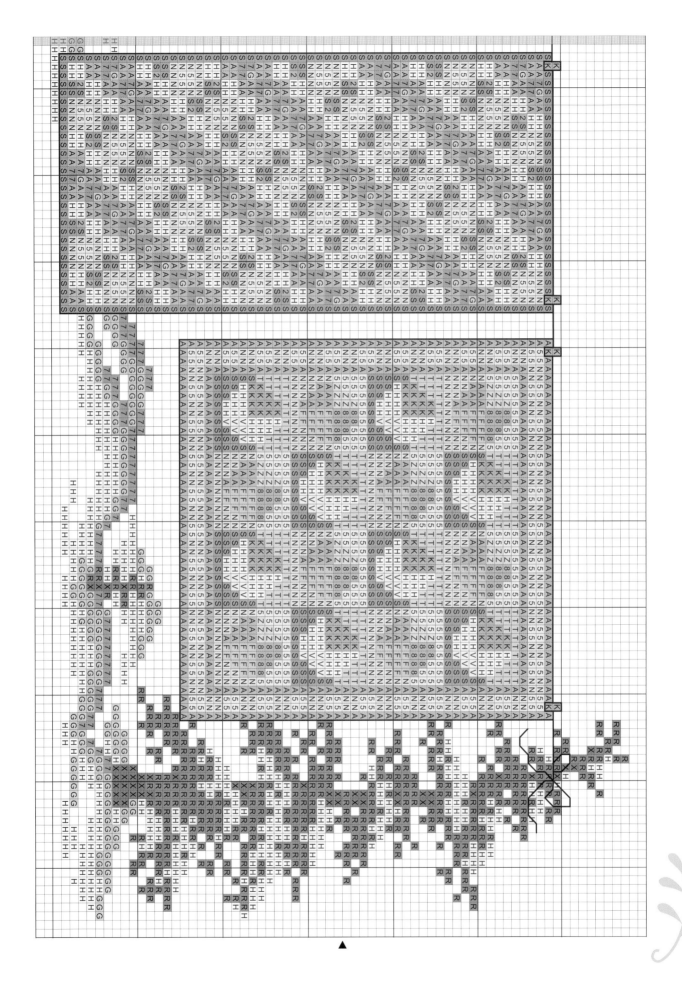

Holiday Quilts

Celebrate the beauty of patchwork quilts with this festive holiday design.

Stitch Count = 291w × 74h

FABRIC SIZE
• One 27" × 10" (68.6cm × 25.4cm) piece of 28-ct. Opalescent White Metallic Jazlyn® by Zweigart® (stitched over two threads)

DESIGN SIZE
• 25-ct. = 23¼" × 6" (59.1cm × 15.2cm)
• 28-ct. = 20¾" × 5¼" (52.7cm × 13.3cm)
• 32-ct. = 18⅛" × 4⅝" (46.0cm × 11.7cm)

▼

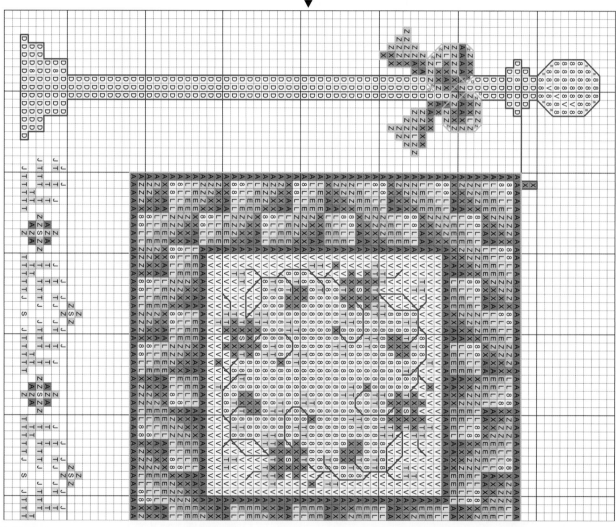

CROSS STITCH				CROSS STITCH				BACKSTITCH			
ANCHOR	DMC		COLOR	ANCHOR	DMC		COLOR	ANCHOR		DMC	COLOR
002	8		White	White	022	A	815	Medium Garnet	403	—	310	Black
019	X	304	Medium Christmas Red	246	N	986	Very Dark Forest Green	022	—	815	Medium Garnet
403	D	310	Black	292	V	3078	Very Light Golden Yellow	246	—	986	Very Dark Forest Green
046	Z	666	Bright Christmas Red	035	E	3705	Dark Melon				
227	T	701	Light Christmas Green	031	L	3708	Light Melon				
238	J	703	Chartreuse	295	S	3822	Light Straw				

Gray area indicates last row of previous section of design.

16

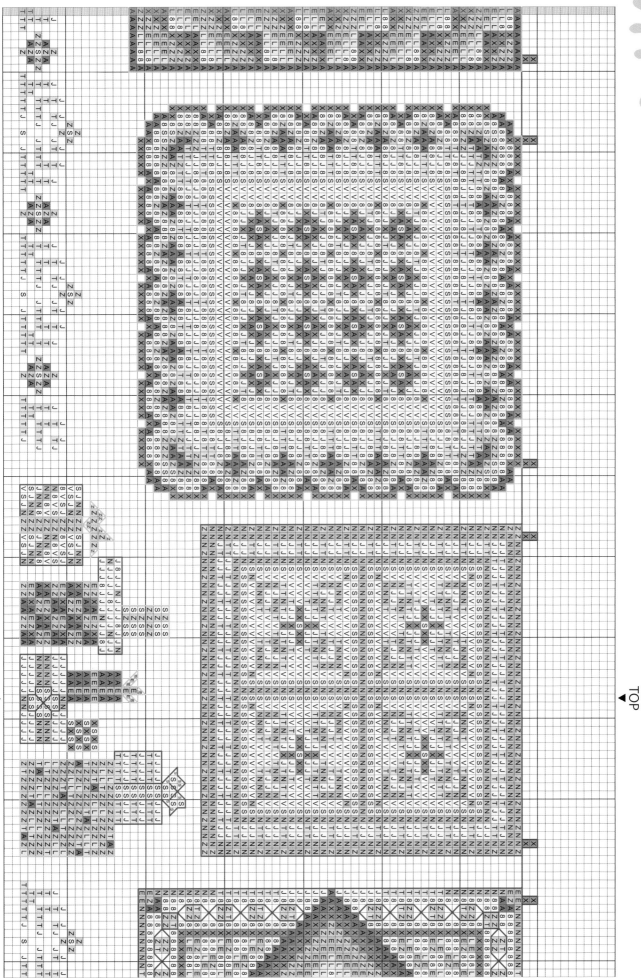

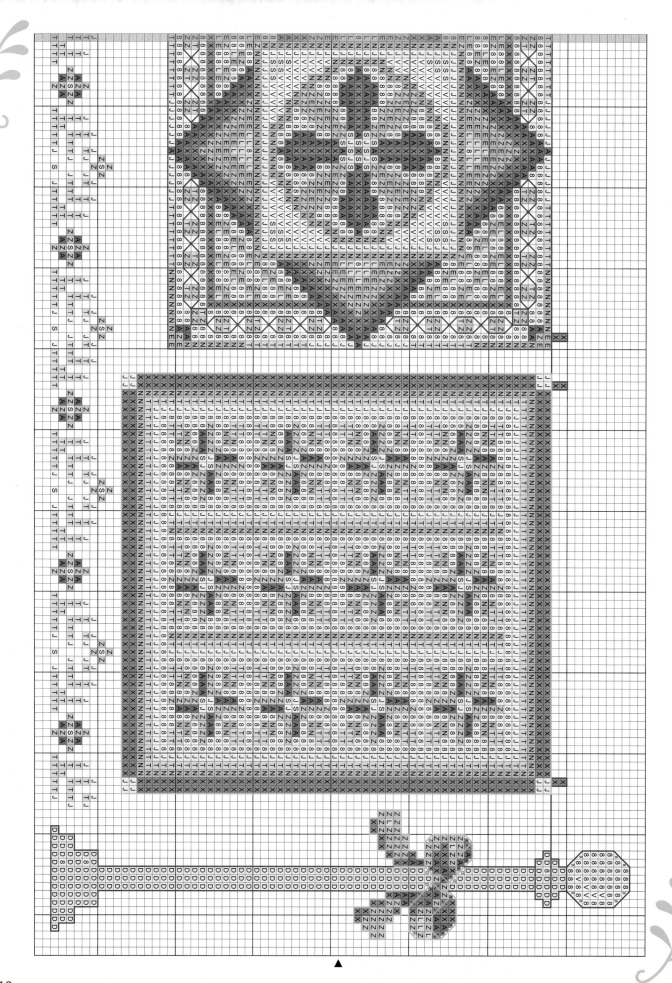